BOSTON UNIVERSITY

Classical Revival molded capital on Bay State Road

BOSTON UNIVERSITY

A Pictorial Commentary

1839 | 1989

BOSTON UNIVERSITY
SESQUICENTENNIAL

Photographs by Steve Dunwell • Preface by Robert V. Bruce

Boston University, Boston 02215

Text © 1989 by the Trustees of Boston University

Photographs © 1989 by Steve Dunwell

All rights reserved. Published 1989

Printed in the United States of America

Library of Congress Cataloging-in-Publication Data

Dunwell, Steve.
  Boston University, a pictorial commentary.

  1. Boston University—Description—Views.   I. Bruce,
Robert V.   II. Title.
LD514.5.D86   1989   378.744'61   88-35263
ISBN 0-87270-064-X (alk. paper)

Preface

BOSTON UNIVERSITY is a school of two rivers, Commonwealth Avenue and the Charles, one glowing by night, one gleaming by day, both flowing in counterpoint through the pages of this splendid book. They define a long, lean campus, straight as a runway cleared for takeoff, and aiming westward like America. The University's flanking streams summon it on the one hand to unhurried reflection, on the other to action. One evokes the oldest Boston, one the newest: the river named for a doomed autocrat now long dead, the avenue named for the good of the people, mortal also, yet ever renewed and so ever alive.

The University, like the universe, is many things to many people. No one knows all of it, yet everyone who has been part of it knows some things about it that others do not. The bright shards of its life and setting that make up the kaleidoscope of this book thus speak differently to each of us through our individual minds and memories. In this preface, therefore, I can only offer a few notions and recollections called up in one man who has frequented this University for more than forty years, yet still finds in Steve Dunwell's masterly photographs a cavalcade of vistas and close-ups, people and things, lights and shadows, colors, shapes, and textures he had never really seen before.

Except for the Schools of Medicine and Graduate Dentistry in the Medical Center off Massachusetts Avenue, all of Boston University's Schools and Colleges are now formed up and dressed down along Commonwealth and the Charles. But when I first came to the University as a graduate student in 1946, fresh from the Pacific theater of World War II,

5

segments of it were still scattered from Beacon Hill to Copley Square. The red-brick building I studied in shared a block with the Renaissance palace of the Boston Public Library, which in its turn shared Copley Square with the elegant Copley Plaza Hotel, Richardson's magnificent Trinity Church, and the imposing church with the seesaw name of New Old South. A block away the solidly dignified Exeter Theater, itself a former church, was running those unforgettable Italian and English movies of the first postwar years — films by Rossellini, De Sica, Reed, Lean. It was a remarkable campus, and when that outpost of the University shifted base a year later to rendezvous with others along Commonwealth Avenue, I had mixed feelings. But I found that the Avenue and the Esplanade doubly link us with Boston's heart, with the Common and the Hill, and so the whole storied city is still our matchless campus, captured here in aerial panorama.

In the life span of the University, the Charles River Campus is new. The first buildings built for it are younger than I am, and most of its present buildings had not yet materialized when I came back to teach only a third of a century ago. Still, one may catch the echo of an earlier age, the first years of this aging century, in the harmonious red-brick bowfronts of Bay State Road, predating the campus but now mostly incorporated in it. Poignant memories haunt that street. There in what is now Shelton Hall, Eugene O'Neill, tragic playwright of New England, the sea, and city life, died in 1953. Long before that, in the stone mansion now called the Castle, a real-life tragedy had its first act. Built for William Lindsay, writer, actor, patron of drama, and munitions millionaire, it was the setting in 1915 for the April wedding of his daughter Leslie to her English fiancé. On page 103 we see part of the Great Hall and the massive staircase from which she tossed her bridal bouquet. En route to England the newlyweds perished when the *Lusitania* was torpedoed and sunk. To Leslie's stricken father the mansion seemed ever after like a mausoleum, but it knows youth and hope again as one center of University life.

Time makes tradition. Our Special Collections library has its early medieval texts and fifteenth-century incunabula, but also its unsurpassed assemblage of twentieth-century manuscripts, someday to ripen into a later century's rich and venerated heritage. The Eiffel Tower, when new, was denounced as a desecration of the Paris skyline; now it spells "Paris" to the world. Likewise the Citgo sign in Kenmore Square has become a visual tradition, restored with the help of the University. Its scarlet rhythms vitalize the night sky as viewed from my office window. By day and night the Prudential building and the John Hancock tower dominate the same view. They will yet become high-rise keepsakes, emblems of a proud past, and so will the most sleekly modern buildings in these pages — until, like the old building at Copley Square, they give way to newer still.

Buildings are only shells. They must be filled with life. And these are. Its teachers and students are the University's true monument and pride. Some have made lives that tower above anything built of stone or steel. Martin Luther King, Jr. (Graduate School '55), is the only American university graduate to be commemorated with a national holiday. In Marsh Chapel Plaza the passerby's spirit is lifted with the rising flight of birds transfixed in Sergio Castillo's King memorial sculpture, *Free at Last*. Edward Brooke (Law '48), remains the only black man to be elected a United States senator since Reconstruction. The University has also produced such widely known graduates as Norman Vincent Peale (Theology '24), Barbara Jordan (Law '59), and F. Lee Bailey (Law '60). In some fields, achievements tend to outstrip celebrity. How many know, for example, that Rebecca Lee Dorsey (Medicine 1883) became the first woman endocrinologist, or that George Lythcott (Medicine '43) led in eradicating smallpox in much of the African continent? It is our alumni in sports, the arts, and politics who are most likely to win wide public recognition — sports heroes like Mickey Cochrane and Harry Agganis; winners of Olympic gold like the runner Dave Hemery and the B.U. foursome, Eruzione, Craig, Silk, and O'Callahan, who powered the U.S. hockey team to victory over the Soviets in 1980; Academy Award winners like Harold Russell, Estelle Parsons, Faye Dunaway, and Olympia Dukakis; journalists like correspondent John Scali, photographers Carl Mydans and Stan Grossfeld, and columnist Mike Barnicle; United States senators like Thomas McIntyre of New Hampshire and William Cohen of Maine; or reformers like Anna Howard Shaw (Medicine 1886), one of the great leaders of the women's rights movement. Faculty too have won fame, from Alexander Graham Bell, who helped unite the human race, to Elie Wiesel, witness and chronicler of its mad self-mutilation in the Holocaust.

And so the honor roll goes on. Alumni and faculty have piled up their Pulitzer and Nobel Prizes, their political offices, their professional honors, their books, poems, films, and plays, their triumphs in medicine, public health, science, technology, music, art, communications, education, social work, business, and law.

But to make a university truly great, such things must rise from a broad, solid base of talented, striving, humane, and honorable students. Boston University has such a base. We see in these pages its students' faces and forms in thought and action: cogitating at a computer keyboard, bent over books and bent on their mastery, absorbed in and absorbing the dialogue of a classroom, exploring the possibilities of canvases and musical instruments, probing the secrets of life, energy, and matter in laboratories, making a joyful noise in concerts, creating worlds on the stage. We see them exultantly testing the limits of their strength and skill in hockey, football, crew, and other sports. We cannot read their minds or measure their prowess from these photographs, but we sense that in time we may read about and measure what those minds and skills have achieved.

In the images of this book there also beats the pulse of the seasons. Even an urban university acknowledges that rhythm. In summer session Boston University has its patches of greenery, its vest-pocket parks, verdant nodes in the network of campus life. They are small, but the Japanese have taught us in their bonsai gardens to see much in little, a prairie in a blade of grass, a forest in a leaf. And those not content with tokens may cross the pedestrian bridge that vaults over the millrace of Storrow Drive and "invite their souls" on the turf of the Esplanade, surveying the sweep of the Charles River Basin, the skyline of Beacon Hill, and the towers beyond, or perhaps looking across to the Cambridge shore and pondering the occult significance of the Hyatt Regency Hotel's homage to Babylonian ziggurats. Here and there on campus the ivy climbs, softening and greening brick and stone walls, and in the chill of autumn warming them with the ripple and shimmer of flame-red leaves.

Winter needs no foliage to show its hand. With its soft comforter it clothes the bare branches, the streets and sidewalks of Commonwealth and Bay State, the ornate carvings of entablatures, lintels, balustrades, and pediments, and the broad frozen surface of the Charles. The city may sully it, but we slog through the slush of February and March, and spring comes round again. Magnolias blossom on Bay State Road. Green leaves beckon through library windows. The programmed response of youth to springtime fills the lawn outside with lollers and the sidewalks with promenaders.

Finals come for all, and then commencement for the seniors. Diplomas are set out in serried tubes, robes sway and flutter in the academic procession at Nickerson Field, speeches are nobly delivered and politely endured, the graduates are pronounced ready to commence, cheers rise, snapshots are taken, families cluster, and farewells are made. The University remains to begin another cycle.

Vicissitudes have come upon it through the years, and have been weathered. The great Boston Fire of 1872 destroyed the downtown buildings of Isaac Rich's bequest, the greatest single donation given any American university to that time, and the insurance companies promptly went under. It was well that the benefactor's name had not also been given to the University. It would have been inappropriate. Close on the fire came the great depression of the 1870s, and others as bad in the 1890s and 1930s. The last one brought merciless salary cuts and belt-tightenings. The two World Wars shrank enrollments frighteningly until students in uniform and subsequent veterans, like myself on the GI Bill, restored them. The antiwar student protests of the 1960s disrupted the campus now and then. I recall looking down from my office window at a maelstrom of shouting students and hard-pressed police on Bay State Road. That time too has passed, though Boston University students are still not reliably prostrate before authority — issues aside, a healthy thing, since unchallenged power tends to corrupt and life needs something to push against. Besides, like the jangle and clatter of Green Line trolleys under classroom windows, an occasional disturbance rouses us to the real world outside.

So Boston University still stands — or rather, runs — between the ruminating river and the rushing avenue, an avenue fitly named Commonwealth, for it bears a treasure that belongs to all.

Now commencement is at hand for the reader. Let the pictures speak.

ROBERT V. BRUCE
Professor of History Emeritus
Boston University

Copper-mullioned wall lanterns — School for the Arts   *Opposite:*   River and sky at first light

Coordinators at Fall Orientation

Information table at Fall Orientation

Moving in

Federal Revival row houses on Bay State Road   *Opposite:* The University in perspect

Scholarly diligence

Marsh Chapel and the tower of the School of Theology
through an autumn window

Overleaf: Autumn ivy —
the President's Office

21

In focus

Commonwealth Avenue promenade

Shared insights — Mugar Memorial Library

Libri antiqui   *Overleaf:* Special Collections, Mugar Library

The Boston University Coat of Arms, Marsh Chapel Plaza

Professor Emeritus Warren O. Ault and student

University Professor Elie Wiesel teaching and learning

Free at Last by Sergio Castillo, a tribute to Martin Luther King, Jr. (Graduate School '55)

Molded embellishment, 226 Bay State Road

Getting off the water

Overleaf: An eight on the Charles

The Head of the Charles Regatta

Piccolo player — Homecoming weekend

Rhett, the Terrier mascot

"Charleston on the Charles" — Homecoming Parade theme, 1988

Cheerleaders' pyramid

Boston University Terriers, 23
New Hampshire Wildcats, 21

Overleaf:
A good moment at the game

The refinement of an idea

The lawyer's brief

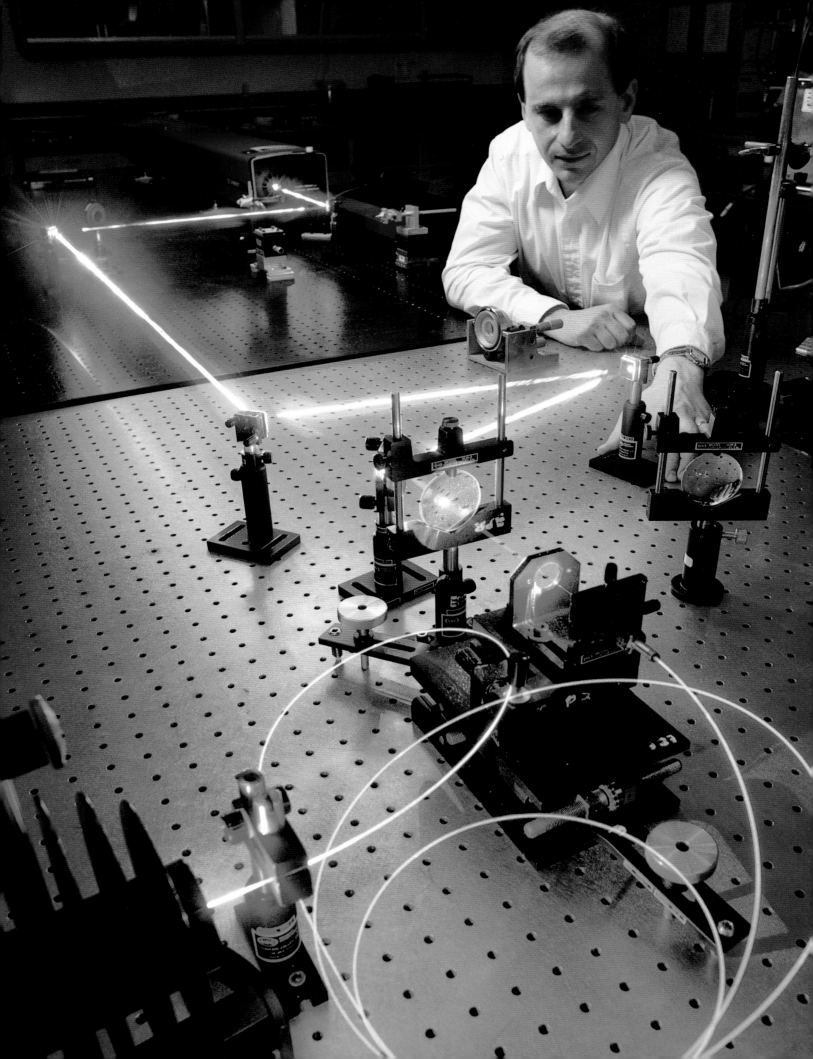

posite: The Laser Laboratory

Boston from Kenmore Square

Late afternoon light outside Warren Towers

Commonwealth Avenue in winter

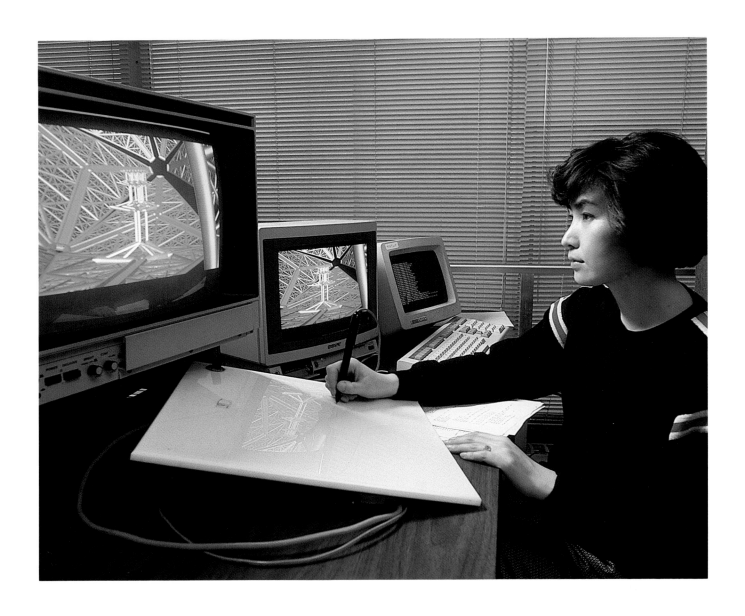

The inspiration of computer graphics

The tower of the College of Liberal Arts at dusk

Overleaf: Collage

53

The Boston Colloquium for the Philosophy of Science

Listening

Suggesting

Discussing

Marsh Chapel with evergreens   *Overleaf:* Making progress

59

Frozen brilliance

Winter lace

Faculty/staff holiday party

A seasonal feast

Assuming a role

A Midsummer Night's Dream — School of Theatre Arts

David Hoose conducts
the Boston University Symphony Orchestra

Opposite
Faculty member Pete
Zazofsky perform:
with the Orchestr

68

The Orchestra at
Symphony Hall,
Boston

Evening colors — Sargent College of Allied Health Professions

The Muir String Quartet, winner of the Naumberg Award,
in residence at Boston University

Overleaf:
Mid-winter shadows

Skiing the Esplanade

Fresh snow; Gothic forms

Pigeonholes — College of Communication

Foreign language mastery — the Geddes Language Center

Overleaf:
The 1988 Beanpot
Tournament

The University Pep Band

Full concentration

Overleaf:
Benefit for the Anthony Spinazzola
Memorial Scholarship Fund

Modern Gothic facade of the Charles Hayden Memorial

Sunlight, arches, and black tie

April forsythia

Almost spring

The organic chemistry laboratory

A tradition of diversity and equality

Players and shadows

A moment of relaxation — intramural field hockey

Overleaf:
The prospect of magnolias

Magnolia stellata — Bay State Road

Stairway and skylight — the Visitors' Reception Center

Balconies and flowers — the President's Office

Scrolled bracket — balcony detail

Campus tour

The Castle, 225 Bay State Road

The Castle: Great Hall fireplace detail

The Great Hall

Overleaf: The Boathouse dock

The long view on Commonwealth Avenue

Cramming

The B.U. Bookstore Mall with banners

Spring afternoon — George Sherman Union

posite: Radiology viewing room   Match Day — School of Medicine

Talbot Building, The University Hospital: Insignia of the Massachusetts Homeopathic Hospital, 1855–1929

Atrium Pavilion, The University Hospital

Young Artists Orchestra, Boston University Tanglewood Institute

Midsummer light

Esplanade, river, and Boathouse

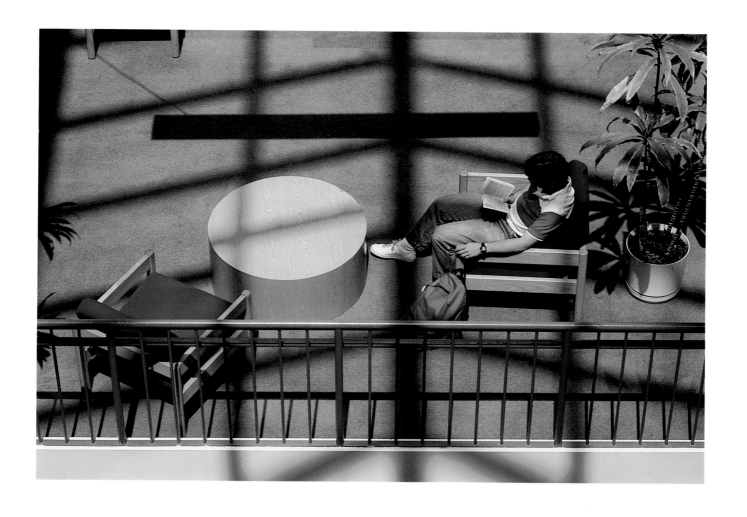

Study lounge in the Arthur G. B. Metcalf Center
for Science and Engineering

Overleaf:
Explosion by Sergio
Castillo, centerpiece
of the Metcalf Center

117

Interactive learning

Atrium and plaza view, the Metcalf Center

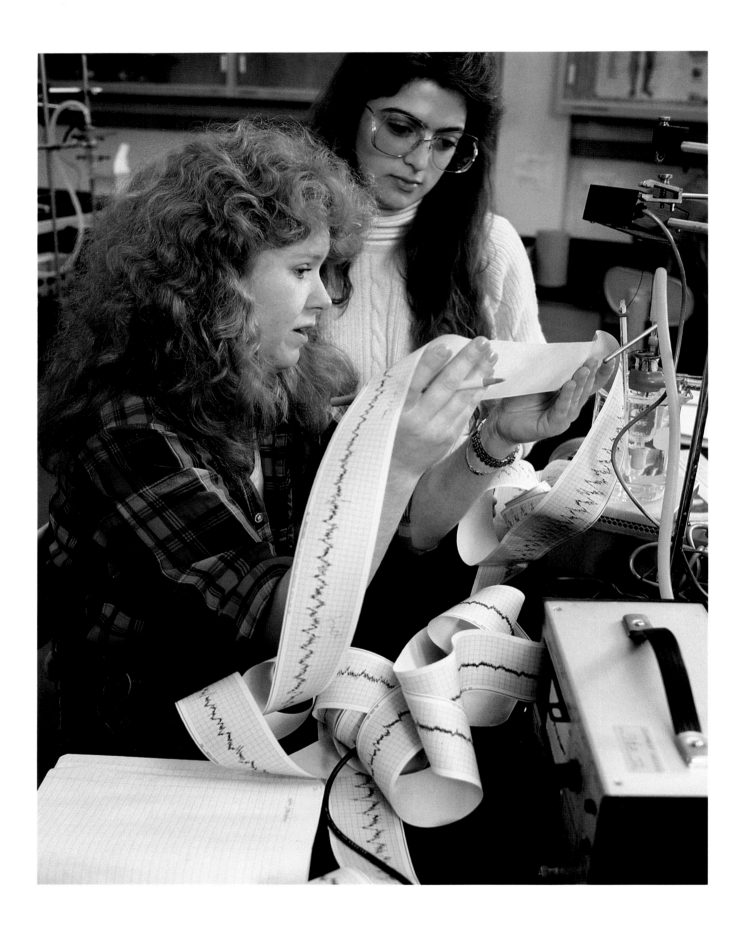

Interpreting data in the biology laboratory

The Academic Computing Center

Overleaf: Clarity of thought

The Boston University Alumni Band

Alumni brass

Commissioning

Baccalaureate Service, Marsh Chapel

Evidence of accomplishment

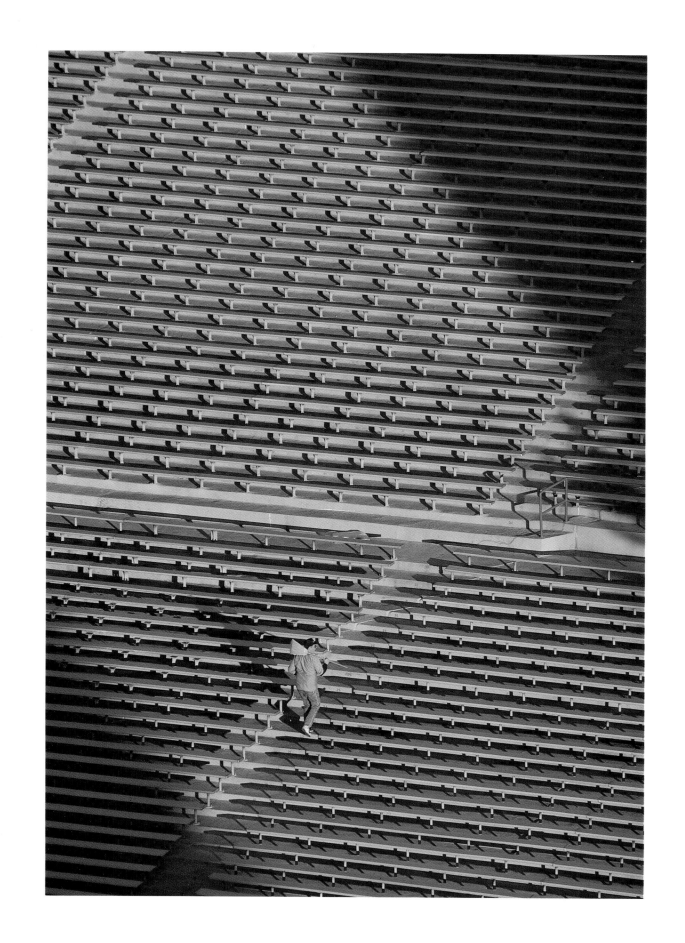

Making ready

Proud parents

A personal message

Waiting

Pomp and Circumstance

Overleaf: Filing in

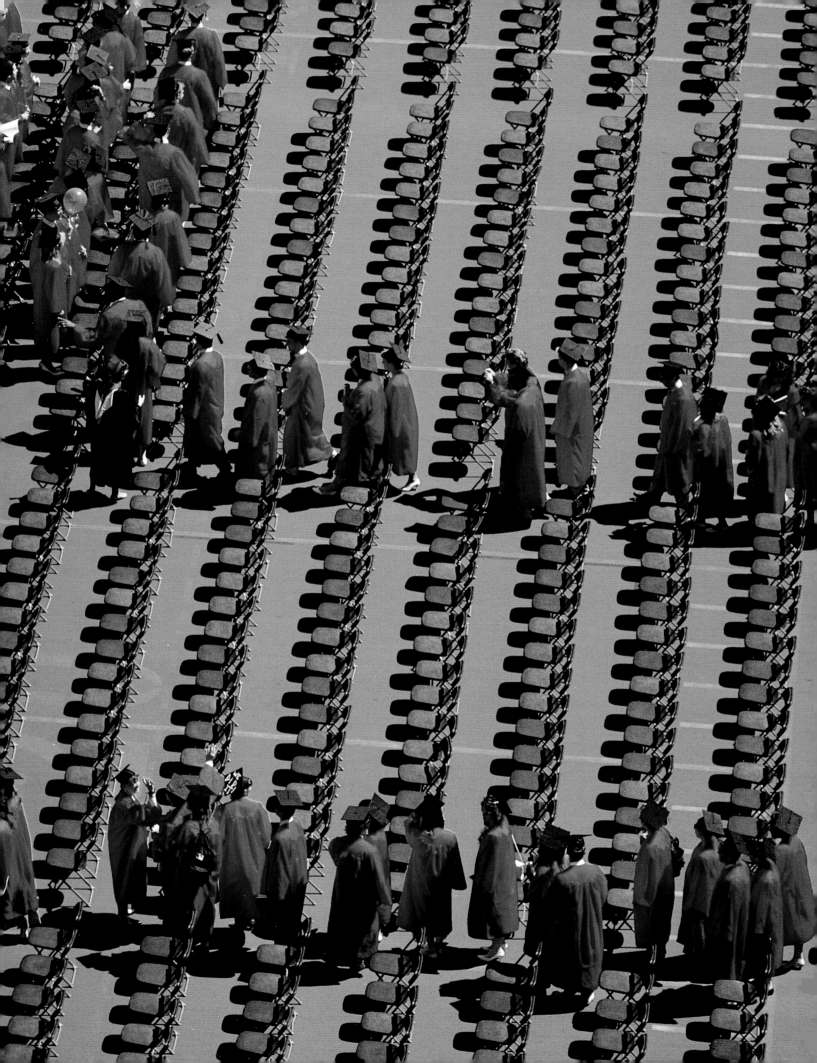

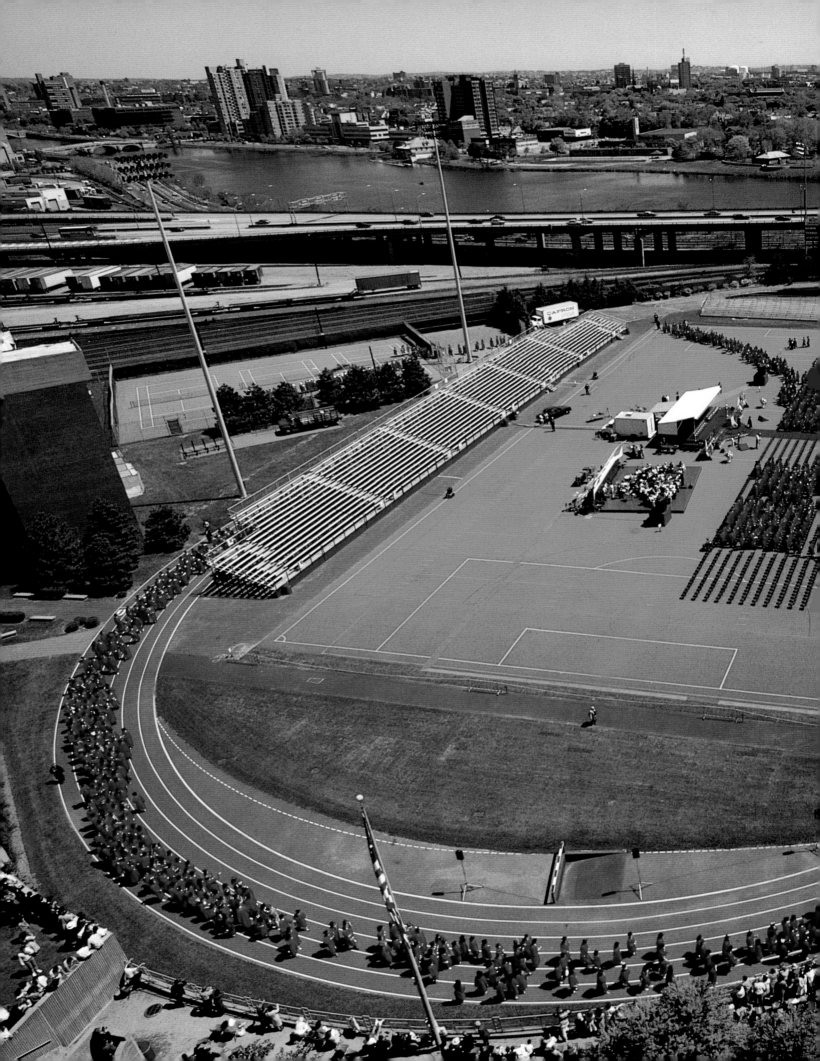

President John Silber at the podium, introducing
honorary degree recipient An Wang at Commencement, 1988

Reviewing the program

Graduates in regalia

Capturing the moment

Literary motif—the Stone Science Building